BOMBS AND BLACKBERRIES

A World War Two play

Julia Donaldson

For my mother – J.D.

ABOUT THE AUTHOR

Julia Donaldson is the author of the award-winning picture book *The Gruffalo*, as well as many other books for children. She is a prolific songwriter, especially for BBC Children's TV programmes, and she has written many plays for a variety of educational publishers for use in schools.

BOMBS AND BLACKBERRIES

A World War Two play

Julia Donaldson

Illustrated by Philippe Dupasquier

an imprint of Hodder Children's Books

The author would like to thank Audrey Jones for her help with this play.

Text copyright © Julia Donaldson 2003
Illustrations copyright © Philippe Dupasquier 2003

'Run, Rabbit, Run'. Music by Noel Gay. Words by Noel Gay and Ralph Butler, 1939.
Noel Gay Music Company Limited (66.67%)/Campbell Connelly & Company Limited,
8/9 Frith Street, London W1 (33.33%). Used by permission of Music Sales Ltd. All
Rights Reserved. International Copyright Secured.
'Chew, Chew, Chew' by Ella Fitzgerald © Copyright 1939 by Exclusive Music
Publications Inc (Publishing) & Warner Bros Publications US Inc (Print). Sole agent for
the UK, British Commonwealth (ex Canada), Norway, Denmark, Sweden and Finland:
Lafleur Music. Reproduced by permission of Boosey & Hawkes Music Publishers Ltd
'Yes! We have no Bananas'. Words and Music by Frank Silver and Irving Conn © 1923,
Skidmore Music Co Inc, USA. Reproduced by permission of EMI Music Publishing Ltd,
London WC2H 0QY.

Editor: Gill Munton
Designer: Don Martin

Published in Great Britain in 2003
by Hodder Wayland, an imprint of
Hodder Children's Books

A catalogue record for this book is available from the British Library.

ISBN: 0 7502 4124 1 (hb)

Printed and bound in Hong Kong by Shek Wah Tong

Hodder Children's Books
A division of Hodder Headline Limited
338 Euston Road, London NW1 3BH

INTRODUCTION

It is September 1939. War has been declared, and a German invasion is feared. Millions of children from British towns are being herded to railway stations, to be taken to the greater safety of the countryside.

The play follows the fortunes of the Chivers family from Manchester during the first two years of the Second World War. Although the family and the other characters are fictional, the play is based on the facts of the Manchester evacuation and the Christmas Blitz of 1940.

Most of the six scenes are set in Manchester and in the Cheshire village to which the three youngest Chivers children are evacuated. There is also a scene in an army hospital in Egypt, where the eldest son is wounded.

The play is intended for reading in class in one or two sessions. There are 29 speaking parts: 14 for girls, 14 for boys and one (the wireless voice) for either a girl or a boy. Additional children could appear in the railway carriage, street and playground scenes, joining in with the chants, games and songs.

The play can, however, be read in small groups, with some children taking more than one role. This can be arranged on a scene-by-scene basis; the characters who appear in each scene are listed at the beginning.

THE CAST

Name	Description	Role
Manchester people		
Mr. Percy Chivers (aged 44)		Large
Mrs. Hilda Chivers (aged 42)	His wife	Large
Stanley (aged 18)		Large
Doris (aged 17)		Large
Elsie (aged 11)	Their children	Large
Jack (aged 9)		Large
Joey (aged 5)		Large

THE CAST

Mr. Biggs		Medium
Brian (aged 10)	} His sons	Large
Charlie (aged 8)		Medium
Mrs. Dawson	A shopkeeper	Medium
Vera (aged 9)	} Her daughters	Small
May (aged 8)		Small
Kenny Larkin (aged 10)	A schoolboy	Small
Miss Oldham	A teacher	Medium

Country people

Mrs. Smiley	The parish clerk	Medium
Mrs. Huggins		Medium
Sally Huggins (aged 11)	Her daughter	Medium
Farmer Gregg		Medium
Albert	The chauffeur at Kite Hall	Small
Miss Skelton	The housekeeper at Kite Hall	Medium

Eileen		Small
Norma	Children in the	Small
Harry	village school	Medium
George		Small

Italian prisoners of war

Luigi (aged 21)		Medium
Paolo (aged 21)		Medium
Nurse Christine	An army nurse	Medium
Wireless voice	(Male or female)	Small

SCENE 1 *Farewell, Manchester*
Autumn 1939

(Miss Oldham, Joey, Elsie, Jack, Doris,
Mr. Chivers, Mrs. Chivers, Brian, Stanley;
non-speaking parts: Charlie, Vera, May)

*A railway carriage in a Manchester station.
Seven Manchester children and their teacher,
Miss Oldham, are squashed on to the seats.
The children are **Elsie, Jack** and **Joey Chivers**;
Brian and **Charlie Biggs**; **Vera** and **May**
Dawson. They have labels on their coats, gas
masks in boxes round their necks, and rucksacks
at their feet.*

SCENE 1

Miss Oldham: Ready, children? One, two, three, four!

Children: *(Singing)*

Fare-well, Man-ches-ter! No - ble town, fare - we - ell!

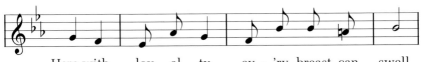

Here with loy - al - ty ev - 'ry breast can swell.

Where - so - e'er I roam, here, as in a home,

Ev - er, dear Lan - ca - shire, my heart shall dwell.

Joey: *(Standing up and looking out of the window)*
Our mam's crying! Elsie! Jack! Our mam's crying!

Elsie: Sit down, Joey.

Joey: Why is she crying? Doesn't she want us to have a
holiday in the country?

Jack: Sit down!

Miss Oldham: Yes, sit down like everyone else, Joey.
You've already said goodbye to your mam.

(Joey sits down. A whistle sounds.)

Jack: We're off!

SCENE 1

*(**Joey** jumps up again.)*

Joey: Bye bye, Mam!

Miss Oldham: Sit down!

*(**Joey** takes no notice. The **other children** jump up and jostle each other at the window.)*

Children: Goodbye! Goodbye!

Miss Oldham: Sit down! *Sit down!*

(The children sit down and "freeze".)

*The Chivers' home. **Mr. Chivers** enters, carrying a rusty helmet with a geranium growing in it. He removes the geranium and starts to scrub the helmet. Enter **Doris**, wearing a nurse's uniform.*

Doris: *(Singing)* "Chew, chew, chew your bubblegum…" Oh, hello, Dad. What are you doing?

Mr. Chivers: What does it look like?

Doris: It looks like you're trying to kill that geranium. Put it back in the flowerpot, Dad.

Mr. Chivers: That's no flowerpot. That's me helmet, that is.

Doris: Yes, I know, but it's been a flowerpot for years.

Mr. Chivers: It did me for the last war, and it'll do me for this one.

Doris: Don't be daft, Dad! You're too old to fight.

Mr. Chivers: That's as maybe, but I don't want a lump of shrapnel in me skull when I'm putting out fires, do I? Don't want a chimneypot braining me when I'm digging folks out of the rubble.

Doris: What's that supposed to mean?

Mr. Chivers: It means I'm joining the fire service.

*(Enter **Mrs. Chivers**.)*

Doris: Hello, Mam. Are the kiddies away, then?

Mrs. Chivers: Aye, they're away … and I nearly jumped on the train with them. Our Joey's little face when they were singing that song!

(She sniffs and gets out her hanky.)

Mr. Chivers: They'll be all right, Hilda love.

Mrs. Chivers: I just hope they'll stick together. I've told Elsie and Jack they must stick together and keep Joey with them.

Doris: Of course they'll stick together.

Mrs. Chivers: It's so awful not knowing how long they'll be away. Suppose this war goes on as long as the last one?

Mr. Chivers: It won't. We'll have Hitler licked in no time.

Mrs. Chivers: What are you doing, Percy? Put that geranium back in the flowerpot.

Mr. Chivers: It's not a flowerpot, it's a helmet. It did me for the last war and it'll do me for this one.

Mrs. Chivers: Don't be stupid, Percy. They'll give you a new helmet. Honestly, you and your crackpot ideas!

Mr. Chivers: Not crackpot, Hilda – crack*helmet!*

*(**Mr. Chivers** laughs at his own joke and exits. **Mrs. Chivers** and **Doris** "freeze".)*

11

SCENE 1

*The railway carriage. **Joey** is holding a little wooden horse to the window and making clip-clop noises.*

Joey: Look, Clopper, a station. What station was that, Elsie?

Elsie: I don't know. They've painted out all the names. It's to confuse the Germans.

Joey: I don't want the Germans to come.

Jack: It's all right, Joey. They won't get far. We'll set traps for them.

Brian: Don't talk so loud, Jack Chivers. Some of them are here already. They're all disguised as nuns and monks.

Jack: Don't be daft, Brian Biggs. Can you see any nuns and monks on this train? It's full of schoolkids.

Brian: What about the guard? He could be a spy. He's got yellow hair.

Jack: So what?

Brian: So, the Germans have all got yellow hair. Don't you know anything, Jack Chivers?

Jack: Yes, I know that you're a daftie.

Miss Oldham: Pipe down, you two. And pull your socks up, Jack. We're nearly there. The tidier you look, the sooner you'll get chosen.

Joey: *(Still holding his horse to the window)* Horses! Look, Clopper, horses! They're going to fight in the war, like you!

Brian: No, they're not! You don't get horses in the war.

Joey: Yes, you do. Our dad said so. He was in the war.

Brian: That was a different war.

Joey: Well, Clopper's going to be in this war. Clopper's a war horse.

Brian: *(To Jack)* Your little brother's as daft as you.

Miss Oldham: Don't start that again, you two. How about another song, everyone? How about "Run, rabbit, run?"

Children:

Run, rab-bit, run, rab-bit, run, run, run.

Don't give the far-mer his fun, fun, fun.

He'll get by with-out his rab-bit pie. So

Run, rab-bit, run, rab-bit, run, run, run.

*(The **children** "freeze".)*

SCENE *1*

The Chivers' home.

Mrs. Chivers: It feels so quiet without them.

Doris: Come on, Mam, you were always on at them to keep the noise down.

Mrs. Chivers: I know – and now I miss it.

*(Enter **Stanley Chivers**, singing.)*

Stanley: "There's something about a soldier, there's something about ..." Oh, hello, Mam.

Mrs. Chivers: Why aren't you at work, Stan?

Stanley: I didn't go in to Metrovick. I've been down to the recruiting office.

Mrs. Chivers: What? You've never joined up! *(Sitting down)* Oh, Stan, what a moment to pick!

14

Doris: Did you pass the medical, Stan?

Stanley: Aye, I'm fighting fit! I'm off tomorrow!

Doris: Tomorrow! What, off to France?

Stanley: No, not to France. I've got to go to a training centre first.

Mrs. Chivers: Oh, Stan, why couldn't you wait to be called up? After all, you'd be helping just as much by staying on in your job. We all know Metrovick is making weapons and suchlike.

Stanley: Look, Mam, I've had an idea. You could get a job with Metrovick yourself! They're opening that new machine shop next month. They'll be looking for tons of workers.

Doris: What are they going to be making, Stan?

Stanley: It's hush-hush.

Mrs. Chivers: I might just do that. It'll get me away from this hush-hush house.

SCENE 2 *The "vackies"*
Autumn 1939

(Farmer Gregg, Mrs. Smiley, Joey, Jack, Sally, Elsie, Mrs. Huggins, Miss Oldham, Vera, May, Albert, Eileen, George, Norma, Harry, Charlie, Brian)

*The village hall. **Miss Oldham**, **Elsie**, **Jack**, **Joey**, **Brian**, **Charlie**, **Vera** and **May** are sitting around looking tired. **Mrs. Smiley** is bustling about. Enter **Farmer Gregg**.*

Farmer Gregg: Have you got three strong, sturdy lads?

Mrs. Smiley: This isn't a cattle market, Mr. Gregg.

Farmer Gregg: I know it's not – I've got plenty of cows. It's cow*boys* I'm short of! *(He points at **Brian** and **Charlie**)* These two will do. *(Pointing at **Jack**)* And maybe this one with the tumbledown socks. I bet you lads don't even know where milk comes from.

Joey: I do! It comes from a jug.

Farmer Gregg: See what I mean? Right, you three, you come along with me.

Jack: Excuse me, mister … I can't. I promised our mam we'd stay together.

Farmer Gregg: I'll just take the two, then.

Mrs. Smiley: Very well. I'm sure you'll be happy on the farm, boys. The fresh air will do you good.

*(**Brian** and **Charlie** exit with **Farmer Gregg**. **Sally Huggins** enters, out of breath, with a bag of apples.)*

Sally: Hello, Mrs. Smiley. I've brought some apples for the vackies.

Mrs. Smiley: You shouldn't call them that, Sally – but I'm sure they'll like the apples.

*(**Sally** hands out the apples.)*

Sally: *(To **Elsie**)* What's your name?

Elsie: Elsie.

Sally: Here's an apple, Elsie. It's from our garden.

Elsie: Thank you. Do you want a currant bun? *(She gets one out of her bag)* Sorry it's a bit squashed.

Sally: Mmm, it's scrummy.

*(Enter **Mrs. Huggins**.)*

Mrs. Smiley: Hello, Mrs. Huggins. It's a couple of girls for you, isn't it?

Mrs. Huggins: Yes, please.

Sally: Can we have Elsie, Mam?

Mrs. Huggins: Would you like to come with us, Elsie?

Elsie: I can't. I promised I'd stick with my brothers.

Miss Oldham: How about these two sisters, Vera and May Dawson? Nobody's chosen them yet because May's got asthma.

Mrs. Huggins: Poor little soul. Would you like to come and share with Sally, girls?

Vera and May: Yes, please!

Sally: But they're too little, Mam. I want Elsie!

Mrs. Huggins: You'll see Elsie at school, Sally. Ready, you two? Don't forget your gas masks.

Miss Oldham: See you in school, girls!

*(**Vera** and **May** exit with **Sally** and **Mrs. Huggins**.)*

Mrs. Smiley: The fresh air will do them good.

Joey: What about us?

Mrs. Smiley: Don't worry. I'm sure we'll find someone.

*(Enter **Albert**.)*

Mrs. Smiley: Ah, good afternoon, Albert. Did Lady Ingleby send you?

Albert: Yes. She said she'd take any that were left over.

Mrs. Smiley: You lucky children! You're going to be staying in Kite Hall. It's a very grand house. There's even a billiard room, isn't there, Albert?

Albert: That's where they're going to be sleeping.

Miss Oldham: Well I never! You'll be such toffs you won't want to know your old teacher! Pull your socks up, Jack! Goodbye, and be good.

Children: Goodbye.

(The children follow Albert out.)

Mrs. Smiley: The fresh air will do them good.

The playground of the village school. Harry, Eileen, George, Norma and Sally run on. Harry stands apart from the others.

Eileen, George and Norma: Farmer, farmer, may I cross your field?

Harry: Yes, if you're wearing red.

(George takes a step forwards.)

Eileen, George and Norma: Farmer, farmer, may I cross your field?

Harry: Yes, if you're wearing black.

(Eileen takes a step forwards.)

Harry: You're not wearing black, Eileen Miller.

Eileen: What colour do you think my gas mask bag is, then? It's made of blackout material.

(Enter Elsie, Vera, May, Charlie and Joey. Joey sits sadly down with his horse. The rest approach the country children.)

Vera: Can we play?

Harry: No, you can't. No vackies allowed.

Charlie: Why not?

Eileen: Because you're from Manchester.

George: You're dirty.

Norma: You've all got head lice.

May: No, we have not!

Harry: Well, you can't play, anyway.

Charlie: I'm going to get my big brother on to you. Brian! Brian!

*(Enter **Brian** with **Jack**.)*

Charlie: That boy says we can't play. He says we're all dirty.

Harry: No, I never. It was George who said that.

George: No, I never. It was Eileen.

Brian: Their game looks stupid, anyway. Me and Jack are playing spies. You can play with us, Charlie.

*(Exit **Brian**, **Jack** and **Charlie**.)*

Sally: I vote the Manchester girls can play with us.

Elsie: I'm only playing if my little brother can, too.

Joey: I don't want to.

Norma: Let's get a move on – playtime's nearly over.

Children: Farmer, farmer, may I cross your field?

Harry: Yes, if you've got head lice!

*(No one steps forward. The bell goes.
The **children** run off, some of them laughing.
Elsie leads **Joey** off, with her arm round him.)*

20

SCENE 3 *The blackout*
Autumn – winter 1939

(Mrs. Chivers, Mr. Chivers, Doris, Mr. Biggs)

*The Chivers' home. Enter **Mrs. Chivers**, with a letter, and **Mr. Chivers**.*

Mrs. Chivers: There's another letter from our Elsie.

Mr. Chivers: Let's have a read.

*(**Mr. Chivers** takes the letter and reads aloud.)*

"Dear Mam and Dad,

I am having a nice time in the country. I have only seen Lady Ingleby twice. Mostly we just see the housekeeper, Miss Skelton. Yesterday, me and Sally picked lots of field mushrooms and her mother cooked them …"

Mrs. Chivers: Oh, no! What if they were them poisonous ones?

Mr. Chivers: Of course they weren't. Be quiet and listen:

"… Jack got in a fruit fight with some boys from the village. Miss Skelton was cross with him. Joey is still a bit sad. I think he is homesick. With love from Elsie"

Mrs. Chivers: Poor Joey. I've a good mind to have them back.

SCENE 3

Mr. Chivers: No, Hilda, it's too dangerous.

Mrs. Chivers: Dangerous? Come off it, Percy. How many German planes have you seen? How many fires have you put out?

Mr. Chivers: If we go through all that again we'll both be late for work. *(Picking up his helmet)* Come on.

Mrs. Chivers: If you ask me, the real danger isn't Hitler – it's the blackout.

*(Exit **Mr. and Mrs. Chivers**.)*

*The casualty department of a Manchester hospital. Enter **Doris**, in her nurse's uniform, and **Mr. Biggs**.*

Doris: Hello, Mr. Biggs. The doctor says you've broken your collar-bone.

Mr. Biggs: Aye. Blinking blackout!

Doris: I'll put a sling on it for you. *(**Doris** bandages **Mr. Biggs** while they talk)* You're Brian and Charlie's dad, aren't you? How are they doing on the farm?

Mr. Biggs: They're getting on fine. But you'll never guess what that farmer's been getting our Brian to do.

Doris: Milk the cows?

Mr. Biggs: No – paint white stripes on them! It's because a cow got knocked down by a car the other week. They have the blinking blackout in the country, too. Pointless, if you ask me.

Doris: So, what happened to you?

Mr. Biggs: Well, I were down the Shambles. Do you know the Shambles?

Doris: Yes, it's that old area, isn't it?

Mr. Biggs: Aye, all steps and twisty alleyways. I went down the Shambles for a couple of pints.

Doris: Just a couple?

Mr. Biggs: Well, maybe three or four. Anyway, when I comes out, it's pitch black. No moon at all. And I'd forgotten me torch. Can't get into the habit of using the things. So there I am, hurrying to catch me tram, and I slips up. I reckon I chose the wrong pub.

Doris: Why?

Mr. Biggs: It were called The Slip Inn!

SCENE 4 *Trickling home*
Spring - summer 1940

(Elsie, Jack, Joey, Miss Skelton, Mrs. Dawson, Mrs. Chivers, Brian, Kenny, Stanley)

The garden at Kite Hall. A sheet is pegged out on a washing line.

Elsie: *(Offstage)* Seven, eight, nine, ten. I'm coming!

*(**Jack** hides behind the sheet. **Joey** follows him, holding Clopper.)*

Jack: You can't hide here. This is my place.

Joey: Oh, go on, Jack! Elsie's coming.

Jack: All right, then.

*(There are footsteps. **Miss Skelton**, the housekeeper, removes the sheet and stands holding it.)*

Joey: It's not Elsie – it's Miss Skelton.

Jack: Good afternoon, Miss Skelton.

Miss Skelton: It may be a good afternoon, but it wasn't a very good night, was it?

Jack: What do you mean?

Miss Skelton: I think your little brother knows what I mean. It was another *wet* night, wasn't it, Joey?

Joey: Yes, Miss. I'm sorry, Miss.

Miss Skelton: Do you think I like washing your wet sheets every day while you run about playing hide-and-seek?

Joey: It's not hide-and-seek, it's prisoners and guards. Me and Jack are the escaped prisoners.

Miss Skelton: You've got every convenience at Kite Hall. An indoor flush toilet, running hot water … you don't have those at home, do you?

Joey: No, Miss Skelton.

Miss Skelton: So why don't you make use of them? Are you just too lazy to get out of bed?

Jack: It's not Joey's fault, Miss Skelton. He doesn't want to wet the bed. He's just homesick.

Miss Skelton: Well, there's a cure for every sickness, and I think I've worked out the cure for this one. Show me that little horse of yours, Joey. *(**Joey** holds the horse out and **Miss Skelton** takes it)* You're fond of it, aren't you?

Joey: Yes, Miss Skelton. Can I have Clopper back, please?

Miss Skelton: You can have Clopper back in the morning – as long as your bed's dry.

> *(**Miss Skelton** exits with the sheet and the horse. **Elsie** runs on.)*

Elsie: Found you! Your turn to be the guard, Jack. Come on, Joey.

Joey: I'm not playing any more.

> *(**Joey** walks away sadly, and **Jack** and **Elsie** follow him.)*

25

A grocery shop in Manchester. **Mrs. Dawson** *is behind the counter. Enter* **Mrs. Chivers**.

Mrs. Dawson: Hello, Mrs. Chivers. What can I do for you?

Mrs. Chivers: Just the usual. Here's our ration books. *(Handing them to* **Mrs. Dawson***)* Give us a tin of Spam, too – it'll jazz up the vegetable pie.

Mrs. Dawson: *(Starting to weigh out sugar, butter and bacon)* How about the vegetables? Have you got them?

Mrs. Chivers: Yes – Percy's been growing them on top of the shelter. Digging for victory, like it says in the posters.

Mrs. Dawson: *(Handing the packages to* **Mrs. Chivers***)* Here you are, then – sugar, butter, bacon. And here's your dried egg.

Mrs. Chivers: How I hate that stuff!

Mrs. Dawson: Me, too. The funny thing is, Vera and May like it. They've been having fresh farm eggs all these months but now they say they prefer the powdered kind.

Mrs. Chivers: Are they back home, then?

Mrs. Dawson: Aye, we fetched them back at the weekend. I don't reckon Hitler's going to bother with little old Britain after all. I'm surprised you let your kiddies stay on at Kite Hall. Vera's been telling us about Joey.

Mrs. Chivers: What about him?

Mrs. Dawson: Well … I mean, our May wet the bed for

a couple of weeks, too, but Sally's mother was very understanding. That Miss Skelton sounds a right so-and-so. Fancy taking away his little horse every time he does it!

Mrs. Chivers: I didn't know anything about all this. Elsie and Jack never said anything in their letters.

Mrs. Dawson: No, well, maybe they're not free to. That Skeleton woman probably reads every word they write.

Mrs. Chivers: That does it – they're coming home!

*(**Mrs. Chivers** takes her shopping and exits. **Mrs. Dawson** follows.)*

SCENE 4

*A Manchester street. Enter **Jack** and **Joey** Chivers, **Brian** and **Charlie Biggs**, and **Kenny**.*

Brian: Let's play convoys.

Kenny: How do you play that?

Brian: You all have to line up. Littlest one at the front – that's you, Joey. Now you all squat down. You're a line of tanks. You've got to move forward slowly, and I'm going to bomb you. I'll wrap some sand in my hanky for the bomb.

*(**Jack**, **Joey**, **Charlie** and **Kenny** move forward. **Stanley Chivers** enters, in uniform, looking very tired. No one notices him. **Brian** throws the "bomb". It lands near **Kenny**.)*

Brian: You've been bombed, Kenny. You're out.

Kenny: That's not fair. It didn't hit me.

Brian: No, but it landed near you. It could have exploded and killed you.

Kenny: No, it couldn't.

Stanley: I'm afraid it could. I've seen that happen.

Jack: Stan! *(He turns to the others)* That's my big brother!

Joey: Stan! Stan! Why are you back? Have we won the war?

*(**Joey** and **Jack** run up to **Stanley**. **Brian**, **Charlie** and **Kenny** cluster round.)*

Stanley: No, Joey, we haven't. Not yet.

Kenny: Where have you been?

Stanley: Dunkirk. That's in France.

Joey: Did you come back in a big battleship?

Stanley: No – in a little French fishing boat.
Is Mam home?

Joey: No, she's out at Metrovick.

Jack: She works there now, like you used to. She says she doesn't know what they're making, but I reckon it's a new bomber.

Brian: Shut up, Jack! I keep telling you, walls have ears.

Joey: Do you want to play convoys, Stan?

Stanley: No, I've had enough war for a while. I just want my bed.

*(The game breaks up, with **Stanley**, **Jack** and **Joey** going one way, and **Brian**, **Charlie** and **Kenny** going the other.)*

SCENE 5 *The Christmas Blitz*
Winter 1940-1941

(Mr. Chivers, Joey, Elsie, Mrs. Chivers, Jack, the wireless voice, Doris, Mr. Biggs, Brian, Charlie, Nurse Christine, Stanley)

*The Chivers' home. It is 22 December 1940. Enter **Mrs. Chivers** with a tray of mince pies, and **Mr. Chivers** with his helmet. **Elsie** and **Jack** bring on a Christmas tree, followed by **Joey**. **Jack** starts to wrap presents in brown paper, and **Elsie** starts to decorate the Christmas tree.*

Mr. Chivers: That Christmas tree looks grand, Elsie.

Joey: Let's hang Clopper up! He can be Father Christmas's reindeer.

Elsie: All right, then. Pass us the string, Jack.

*(**Elsie** ties some string round Clopper and hangs him on the tree.)*

Mrs. Chivers: *(Putting the mince pies in the oven)* I'm warning you all – there won't be a cake this year. I've used up the last of the sugar in the mince pies.

Mr. Chivers: Never mind, love. Christmas will still be Christmas, cake or no cake.

Mrs. Chivers: It's not really the cake I'm going to miss. It's our Stanley.

Jack: At least we saw him in the summer, Mam.

Mrs. Chivers: Aye, but then he was off again to Egypt as quick as you can say Jack Robinson.

Mr. Chivers: Don't worry about Stan. I bet he's sitting on top of a pyramid, toasting us all. Cheerio, everyone – see you all in the morning!

*(**Mr. Chivers** puts his helmet on and exits.)*

Mrs. Chivers: Let's put the wireless on – maybe there'll be some nice carols. *(She switches it on)*

The wireless voice: A town in the north-west of England was heavily bombed last night.

Mrs. Chivers: Oh, no! That's really cheered me up! *(She switches the wireless off)*

Jack: Which town was it, Mam?

Mrs. Chivers: Liverpool. The fires were so bad that half the Manchester brigade had to go and help out. They're still there. That's why your dad's got to do this extra duty tonight.

*(Enter **Doris**, looking glamorous.)*

Elsie: You look nice, Doris.

Doris: What do you think of my lipstick?

Elsie: It looks good – but I thought you said you'd no lipstick left?

Doris: I haven't – this is beetroot juice!

Jack: Where are you off to, Doris?

Doris: I'm going to a party at the Eccles first aid post.

(The air-raid siren sounds.)

Doris: Oh, no! An air raid – that's just what I need.

Mrs. Chivers: I doubt it'll last long. They're just passing over on their way to Liverpool. Right, come on, kiddies. Doris, turn off the oven, will you? Elsie, fetch us down a couple of extra blankets – it's going to be a cold night.

*(There is a knock on the door. **Doris** opens it. **Mr. Biggs**, **Brian** and **Charlie** are standing there.)*

Doris: Hello, Mr. Biggs.

Mr. Biggs: We were just wondering, like – do you have any room in your shelter? Ours is flooded.

Mrs. Chivers: Is it just the three of you?

Mr. Biggs: Aye. My Betty's on duty at the rest centre.

Mrs. Chivers: I daresay we can squeeze you in. Ready, everyone?

*(They **all** exit.)*

The air-raid shelter in the Chivers' garden.
***Mrs. Chivers**, **Doris**, **Elsie**, **Jack**, **Joey**, **Mr. Biggs**, **Brian** and **Charlie** are inside it. Several hours have passed. There are sounds of aircraft and gunfire. A plane passes directly overhead.*

Jack: That was a Stuka.

Brian: No, it wasn't – it was a Heinkel.

(There is the sound of a bomb exploding.)

Doris: That was close!

Mr. Biggs: Come on, let's have another song.

SCENE 5

*(**Mr. Biggs** starts to sing and the **others** join in.)*

All:

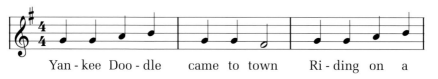

Yan - kee Doo - dle   came to town   Ri - ding on   a

po - ny. He   stuck a   fea - ther   in   his   cap and

called it ma - ca - ro - ni.

Joey: Where's Clopper?

Elsie: He's on the Christmas tree – don't you remember?

Joey: *(Going towards the door)* I'm going to get him.

Jack: Don't be daft, Joey.

Doris: Pass us your book, Joey – I'll read you another story.

Joey: I don't want a story. I want Clopper.

Charlie: Can we have a peep outside, Dad?

Mr. Biggs: *(To **Mrs. Chivers**)* What do you think? Shall we let them?

Mrs. Chivers: All right, then, but put out the torches, everyone.

*(**Mr. Biggs** opens the door and they peer out.)*

Charlie: The sky's all red.

Elsie: What's that on the roof?

Mr. Biggs: By gum! It's a parachute! Keep back, everyone.

*(Exit **Mr. Biggs**.)*

Joey: Where's he going?

Brian: There's a German landed on the roof. Dad's going to catch him.

Charlie: I can't see anyone on the roof.

Elsie: What's that box thing that's dangling down?

Joey: Is it the German's suitcase?

Jack: What? Where? *(He jostles to the front)* There isn't a parachutist – that's a parachute bomb!

Brian: Dad! Stop! Stop!

Mrs. Chivers: Mr. Biggs!

Doris: Come back!

Charlie: *It's a bomb!*

*(**Mr. Biggs** comes back into view. As he approaches the shelter, there is a deafening explosion.)*

An army hospital in Egypt. It is January 1941.
Stanley Chivers, *who has been wounded, is in*
bed. **Nurse Christine**, *an army nurse, enters.*

Nurse Christine: You're a lucky chappie, Gunner
Chivers. You've got two letters. They've been
forwarded from HQ. Shall I sit you up?

Stanley: Just call me Stan. *(He takes the letters)* Ta.
This one's from my mam. *(He starts to read)*

"Dear Stan,

I hope you are keeping safe in Egypt ..."

Oh, no!

Nurse Christine: What's the matter?

Stanley: They've been bombed out. They're in a rest
home. All except my little sister Elsie. She's
gone to stay with her friend in the country.
It sounds terrible – listen to this. *(He reads)*

"There were Christmas cards scattered all over
the garden. Joey was upset about the tree and the
presents getting burned – and that little horse
you made for him."

Nurse Christine: Poor little thing. Did the fire brigade
get there all right?

Stanley: I think so. Yes. Here's what she says.
(He reads)

"Your Dad's lot came, though not as quick as
they might – there were that many fires all over
the city. Doris's hospital was bombed. One bomb
fell down a chimney into a ward full of patients,

35

but Doris's friend put it out by covering it with sand."

Nurse Christine: Good for her! Was Doris on duty, too?

Stanley: No, she was supposed to be going to a party. By golly, listen to this. *(He reads)*

"Thank goodness she didn't make it, because a bomb fell in the road and twelve of them were killed. Our Doris is a bit down in the dumps, but I daresay she'll snap out of it. Hoping for good news of you soon.

Your loving Mother"

Oh, no. *(He lies back in bed)*

Nurse Christine: At least they're all alive, Stan.

Stanley: I know – but now they'll have got the telegram about my leg. How are they going to feel about that?

Nurse Christine: Shall I read you your other letter?

Stanley: Yes, please. I think it's from Jack.

Nurse Christine: Here we go, then. *(She reads)*

> "Dear Stan,
>
> I hope you are still beating the Italians in Egypt. We have had an exciting time. Our house got bombed, and so did loads of others. Me and Brian Biggs have collected tons of shrapnel. Mr. Biggs got a bit burned by a parachute bomb, but he is more fed up about The Slip Inn getting destroyed. Metrovick got bombed, too, so we could all see what they were making. It was a new bomber, just like I said – a bomber called the 'Manchester'!
>
> With love from Jack"

That was a bit jollier.

Stanley: That's kids for you – the war's a big adventure to them.

Nurse Christine: You're not much more than a kid yourself, Stan.

Stanley: Well, I don't feel like one any more.

SCENE 6 *Prisoners of war*
Autumn 1941

(Elsie, Sally, Luigi, Paolo, Farmer Gregg, Kenny, Joey, Charlie, Brian, Jack, Doris, Mrs. Smiley, Mrs. Huggins)

A country field. **Elsie** *and* **Sally** *are collecting rosehips.*

Elsie: I've never tasted rosehip syrup. We never had it when we were little.

Sally: I don't like it much. But it's good for babies.

Elsie: I reckon we've picked enough for an army of babies.

Sally: We'll be getting medals from Mr. Churchill.

Luigi and Paolo: *(Offstage, singing)* "Una rosa da Vienna, Una piccola rosa …"

Elsie: Who's that singing?

Sally: I don't know. It sounds foreign. *(They peep offstage)*

Elsie: Look! It's two men. They're picking Farmer Gregg's apples.

Sally: Do you think they're German invaders?

Elsie: I don't know … I thought Hitler had given up on that idea.

Sally: They've seen us! Shall we run?

Elsie: No – they look quite friendly.

*(Enter **Luigi** and **Paolo** with baskets of apples.)*

Luigi: Buon giorno!

Sally: I think they *are* German.

Paolo: No. No German. Italiano.

Elsie: They're Italian. They've not got any guns.

Paolo: No guns. Prisoners.

Luigi: Very nice prison. Sun, trees. No walls.

Paolo: You want apple?

Sally: No, thank you.

Luigi: Me – Luigi. My friend – Paolo.

Elsie: I'm Elsie. And this is my friend Sally.

Luigi: Elsie. Sally. Very nice names. Very nice girls.

Paolo: You like pupina?

Sally: Pupina – what's that? *(**Paolo** produces a wooden doll)* Oh, it's a doll. That's nice.

Paolo: I make it. Wood, knife.

Elsie: That's really clever.

Paolo: I make for my sister. But you can have.

Elsie: It's all right, Paolo. Me and Sally are too old for dolls. Keep it for your little sister.

Luigi: You have sister also?

Elsie: Not a little one – a big one. But she's in Manchester. Big town.

Luigi: Your big sister pretty like you?

Elsie: She's prettier than me! *(She laughs)*

Luigi: Happy like you?

Elsie: I don't know. She always used to be happy. But then some of her friends got killed in the war. I think she's still sad about that.

Paolo: She come here. Sky, trees. Very nice. She happy again.

Sally: That's a good idea, Elsie. Why don't I ask Mam if Doris can come for a holiday? Maybe Joey could come, too. You and me could camp in the garden.
*(Enter **Farmer Gregg**.)*

Farmer Gregg: What's all this, then? You two are supposed to be picking apples, not chatting up the girls.

Sally: Don't be cross with them, Mr. Gregg. Me and Elsie have got to go now. Goodbye, Luigi! Goodbye, Paolo!

Luigi: Arrivederci!
*(They **all** exit.)*

SCENE 6

A Manchester street. Enter **Jack**, **Brian**, **Charlie**, **Joey** *and* **Kenny**.

Kenny: "Eeny, meeny, Mussolini, Eeny, meeny, out!" You're an Italian, Joey.

Joey: I don't want to be.

Kenny: You've got to be. It's desert sands. You can't play desert sands without any Italians.

Charlie: I'm being Mussolini. Don't you want to be in my army, Joey?

Joey: No! I'm not being Italian! I hate Italians!
(He runs off)

Brian: Your brother's such a baby, Jack. You'd never think he was seven.

Jack: I know. But it's because of our big brother. It was the Italians who gave Stan his wooden leg.

Kenny: My uncle's got two wooden legs.

Brian: No, he has not, Kenny Larkin.

Charlie: Anyway, are we still playing desert sands?

41

Jack: Let's play it on the bomb-site.

*(They **all** run off.)*

*The country field. Enter **Doris**, **Joey**, **Elsie**, **Sally**, **Mrs. Huggins** and **Mrs. Smiley** with a picnic basket. They spread out a rug and sit down.*

Doris: This blackberry jam is lovely. I do like a picnic!

Mrs. Smiley: I can't get over how Joey's grown. Well, Joey, is it nice being back in the country?

Joey: Yes, Mrs. Smiley.

Mrs. Smiley: How about staying on? I'm sure Farmer Gregg would take you in. The fresh air would do you good.

Joey: No, thank you.

Mrs. Huggins: I think he's scared of bumping into that Miss Skelton.

Doris: So, Elsie, what about this surprise you were on about?

Elsie: It's coming soon.

Sally: Here it comes!

*(Sally points at **Luigi** and **Paolo** who enter with a basket.)*

Luigi: Good afternoon.

Elsie: *(Proudly)* Buon giorno! That's "good day" in Italian. This is Luigi and this is Paolo. They're Italian prisoners. This is my little brother Joey, and this is my big sister Doris.

Doris: Hello, there!

Elsie: Say hello, Joey.

42

(Joey pretends not to hear.)

Mrs. Huggins: Maybe he's shy.

Paolo: We bring plums. Many plums.

Luigi: And flowers.

(Luigi gives a bunch of wild flowers to Doris.)

Doris: Thank you. They're beautiful.

Paolo: Your sister tell me you nurse. Now I want to be ill. I go to your hospital.

Joey: You can't. They don't let Italians in.

Doris: Don't be silly, Joey.

Sally: Doris's hospital got bombed, didn't it, Doris?

Doris: Yes, but it's been repaired now.

Luigi: War is sad. Many bombs. Many people kill. Me – two brothers die.

Mrs. Huggins: I am sorry, Luigi.

Paolo: We no want to fight. Our leader, he want. We no want.

Mrs. Smiley: It's a sorry business. Here, have a jam sandwich.

Luigi: Thank you. Very good bread. Good, like Italian bread.

Paolo: I have present for you, Joey. *(He brings a jointed horse out of the basket of plums)* Your sister tell me you like horses. I make for you.

(Paolo holds the horse out to Joey, who doesn't take it.)

Doris: It's lovely! You are clever, Paolo.

(Paolo beams.)

Paolo: Is a dancing horse. I pull string, he dance.

     *(**Paolo** demonstrates. The **others** laugh.)*

Doris: Say thank you, Joey.

Joey: *(Taking the horse)* Thank you.

Paolo: My town – Siena. Many horses – how you say, running quick, quick, quick?

Elsie: Racing? Horse racing?

Paolo: Yes. Horse racing. War finish, you come to Siena, Joey. Bring sisters.

Doris: I sometimes wonder if it will ever finish.

Luigi: Yes, yes. It finish.

Sally: When it does, I know what I want – a pound of flying saucers.

Elsie: *(Explaining to **Paolo** and **Luigi**)* They're a kind of sweet. I want a pound of pear drops.

Joey: I want a pound of liquorice bootlaces.

Doris: A drawer full of stockings will do me. How about you, Paolo?

Paolo: Pasta! Big, big – a mountain!

Luigi: For me, pizza – big, like horse-race place!

Mrs. Smiley: A nice pleated skirt for me.

Mrs. Huggins: And I'll have a crate of bananas!

Everyone: Mmmmmm!

Doris: There's a song about that.

     *(**Doris** starts to sing and the **English people** join in. The **Italians** begin to catch on, and by the end of the song, **Joey** is dancing the horse about.)*

Everyone: *(They sing the song twice)*

YES! We have no ba - na - nas —— We have no ba-

na - nas to - day —— We've string beans and HON-ions, cab-

BAH-ges and scal-lions And all kinds of fruit and say ——

—— We have an old fash-ioned to - MAH-to ——

Long Is - land po - TAH-to —— But YES! we

have no ba - na - nas —— We have no ba - na - nas to -

day.

The End

About the play

The play may be either read in class or performed in front of an audience. It will take about 45 minutes. If you want to create a longer entertainment, you could add some more wartime songs and perhaps present a project on the Second World War.

Although the play has been divided into six scenes, the action moves from place to place within each scene. In total there are eleven locations: a railway carriage, the Chivers' home, a village hall, a playground, a casualty department, the garden of a stately home, a shop, a street, an air-raid shelter, a hospital ward and a field.

Staging

There is no need for an elaborate production; it is probably more effective to keep props and scenery to a minimum.

The washing line in Scene 4 could be used at other points in the play to peg backcloths or props. The Christmas tree in Scene 5 could be made of paper or fabric and pegged on the line.

The children who are acting could also be scene shifters. For instance, the railway carriage in Scene 1 could be created by eight chairs which the actors later lift and scatter around to create the village hall at the beginning of Scene 2.

There are several sound effects in the play: the noises made by trains, planes and bombs, and the twittering of birds in the countryside. Children could either compile a soundtrack or make the noises with instruments or voices.

Scene changes could be indicated by sounds or music. For instance, at the beginning of the scene around the Christmas tree, the characters could enter humming a carol. Alternatively, a child could beat a gong or a drum to indicate a scene change.

If lighting is to be used, a blackout at the "cliffhanger" ending of the air-raid scene would be effective.

Costume

Costumes can be kept simple, too. Most of the characters are quite poor, so some of the clothes could be patched.

Everyone was required to carry a gas mask during the war, so both town and country people should have boxes or bags on strings round their necks.

The schoolboys should wear shorts, not long trousers, and girls' and women's skirts should be knee-length.

Mr. Chivers' helmet could be made of papier mâché.

The two nurses, Albert the chauffeur and soldier Stan do not have to be in full uniform; indications such as appropriate headgear will be enough. Stan could wear pyjamas in Scene 5.

The two Italian prisoners of war could wear boiler suits, and the housekeeper, Miss Skelton, could be dressed in an overall.

Enjoy yourselves!

HODDER WAYLAND PLAYS

If you've enjoyed *Bombs and Blackberries*, try the other titles in the series:

The Head in the Sand by Julia Donaldson

Arthur Godbold digs up a bronze head from a Suffolk river. As he and his friend Gertie puzzle over it, the dramatic story of the Roman invasion of Britain unfolds in front of their very eyes. Emperor Claudius, British Queen Boudicca, Roman soldiers and British slave girls are all involved in this fascinating and exciting story.

Cruel Times by Kaye Umansky

Sissy is doing her best as a kitchen maid to earn the little money on which her Ma and family depend. But when she is robbed by a gang of urchins they face destitution – until she meets Charles Dickens. A tender-hearted story of rich and poor set in Queen Victoria's Britain.

Humble Tom's Big Trip by Kaye Umansky

Humble Tom, a shepherd boy, leaves his country home to see the world. Will he survive the rickety roads, the disgusting diseases, the city crooks and the foul-tasting pottage? This hilarious farce is set in Tudor times around King Henry VIII's voyage to the Field of the Cloth of Gold.

All these books can be purchased from your local bookseller. For more information about Hodder Wayland plays, write to:

The Sales Department, Hodder Children's Books,
A division of Hodder Headline Limited, 338 Euston Road,
London NW1 3BH